To An Awesome Son:

All boys love Easter
bunnies, chocolate, egg games,
and a basket full of goodies!

I hope Easter is egg-citing...
filled with fun and adventure
for an AWESOME SON!

A boy as special as you
should get your favorite
treats from the Easter bunny!

Here's wishing the Easter Bunny brings you the best and most colorful eggs!

HOP! HOP! HOP! The Easter Bunny is on his way to make sure you have plenty of sweet treats!

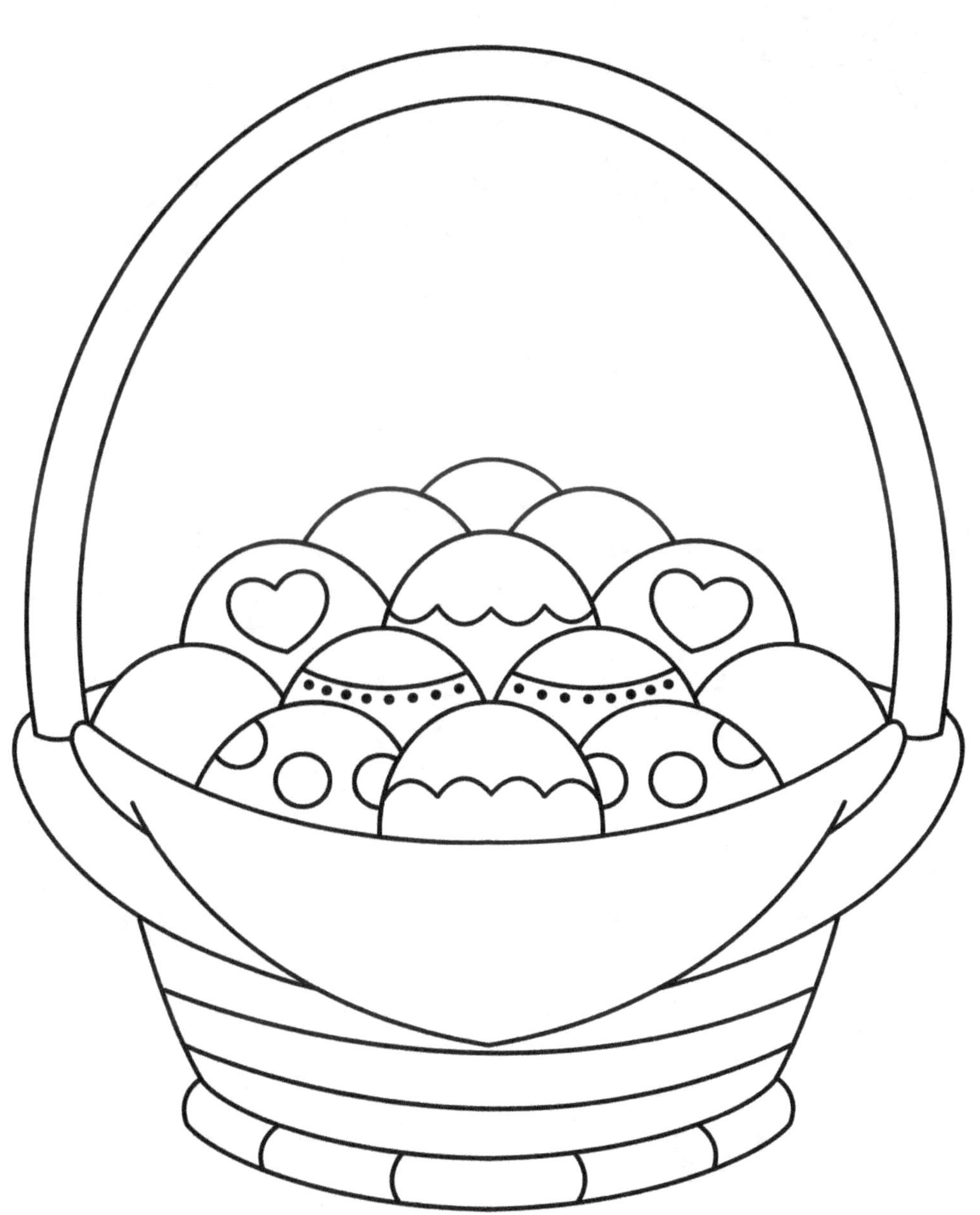

Wishing you a wonderful time as you celebrate Easter with family & friends!

One of the best things about Easter is...
all of the chocolate eggs
boys get to eat!

The Easter Bunny told me that you
are an EGG-STRA
AWESOME SON!

There is no other boy in the world that deserves more fun than you this Easter!

Have a fantastic Easter with plenty of
chirping chickens & fluffy bunnies!

Here's hoping that you have good luck
this year on your Easter egg hunt!

Happy Easter
To My Awesome Son!
(Coloring Card)
(Personalized Card) Easter Messages,
Greetings, & Poems for Children!

May you have a wonderful
holiday and the Easter
Bunny fills your basket with lots
of good things!